Recover,
Bitterness

Dale & Juanita Ryan

6 Studies for
Groups or Individuals

With Notes for Leaders

 *LIFE RECOVERY GUIDES*

INTERVARSITY PRESS
DOWNERS GROVE, ILLINOIS 60515

InterVarsity Press is the book-publishing division of InterVarsity Christian Fellowship, a student movement active on campus at hundreds of universities, colleges and schools of nursing in the United States of America, and a member movement of the International Fellowship of Evangelical Students. For information about local and regional activities, write Public Relations Dept., InterVarsity Christian Fellowship, 6400 Schroeder Rd., P.O. Box 7895, Madison, WI 53707-7895.

All Scripture quotations, unless otherwise indicated, are from the Holy Bible, New International Version. Copyright © 1973, 1978, International Bible Society. Used by permission of Zondervan Bible Publishers.

Cover illustration: Tim Nyberg

ISBN 0-8308-1154-0

Printed in the United States of America

12   11   10   9   8   7   6   5   4
99   98   97   96   95

An Invitation to Recovery

Life Recovery Guides are rooted in four basic convictions.

First, we are in need of recovery. The word *recovery* implies that something has gone wrong. Things are not as they should be. We have sinned. We have been sinned against. We are entangled, stuck, bogged down, bound and broken. We need to be healed.

Second, recovery is a commitment to change. Because of this, recovery is a demanding process and often a lengthy one. There are no quick fixes in recovery. It means facing the truth about ourselves, even when that truth is painful. It means giving up our old destructive patterns and learning new life-giving patterns. Recovery means taking responsibility for our lives. It is not easy. It is sometimes painful. And it will take time.

Third, recovery is possible. No matter how hopeless it may seem, no matter how deeply we have been wounded by life or how often we have failed, recovery is possible. Our primary basis for hope in the process of recovery is that God is able to do things which we cannot do ourselves. Recovery is possible because God has committed himself to us.

Finally, these studies are rooted in the conviction that the Bible can be a significant resource for recovery. Many people who have lived through difficult life experiences have had bits of the Bible thrown at their pain as a quick fix or a simplistic solution. As a result, many people expect the Bible to be a barrier to recovery rather than a resource. These studies are based on the belief that the Bible is not a book of quick fixes and simplistic solutions. It is, on the contrary, a practical and helpful resource for recovery.

We were deeply moved personally by these biblical texts as we worked on this series. We are convinced that the God of the Bible can bring serenity to people whose lives have become unmanageable. If you are looking for resources to help you in your recovery, we invite you to study the Bible with an open mind and heart.

Getting the Most from Life Recovery Guides

Life Recovery Guides are designed to assist you to find out for yourself what the Bible has to say about different aspects of recovery. The texts you will study will be thought-provoking, challenging, inspiring and very personal. It will become obvious that these studies are not designed merely to convince you of the truthfulness of some idea. Rather, they are designed to allow biblical truths to renew your heart and mind.

We want to encourage realistic expectations of these discussion guides. First, they are not intended to be everything-the-Bible-says about any subject. They are not intended to be a systematic presentation of biblical theology.

Second, we want to emphasize that these guides are not intended to provide a recovery program or to be a substitute for professional counseling. If you are in a counseling relationship or are involved in a support group, we pray that these studies will enrich that resource. If you are not in a counseling relationship and your recovery involves long-term issues, we encourage you to consider seeking the assistance of a mental health professional.

What these guides are designed to do is to help you study a series of biblical texts which relate to the process of recovery. Our hope is that they will allow you to discover the Good News for people who are struggling to recover.

There are six studies in each Life Recovery Guide. This should provide you with maximum flexibility in how you use these guides. Combining the guides in various ways will allow you to adapt them to your time schedule and to focus on the concerns most important to you or your group.

All of the studies in this series use a workbook format. Space is provided for writing answers to each question. This is ideal for personal study and allows group members to prepare in advance for the discussion. The guides also contain leader's notes with suggestions on how to lead a group discussion. The notes provide additional background information on certain questions, give helpful tips on group dynamics and suggest ways to deal with problems that may arise during the discussion. These features enable someone with little or no experience to lead an effective discussion.

Suggestions for Individual Study

1. As you begin each study, pray that God would bring healing and recovery to you through his Word.

2. After spending time in personal reflection, read and reread the passage to be studied.

3. Write your answers in the spaces provided or in a personal journal. Writing can bring clarity and deeper understanding of yourself and of the Bible. For the same reason, we suggest that you write out your prayers at the end of each study.

4. Use the leader's notes at the back of the guide to gain additional insight and information.

5. Share what you are learning with someone you trust. Recovery is empowered by experiences of community.

Suggestions for Group Study

Even if you have already done these studies individually, we strongly encourage you to find some way to do them with a group of other people as well. Although each person's recovery is different, everyone's recovery is empowered by the mutual support and encouragement that can only be found in a one-on-one or a group setting. Several reminders may be helpful for participants in a group study:

1. Realize that trust grows over time. If opening up in a group setting is risky, realize that you do not have to share more than what feels safe to you. However, taking risks is a necessary part of recovery. So, do participate in the discussion as much as you are able.

2. Be sensitive to the other members of the group. Listen attentively when they talk. You will learn from their insights. If you can, link what you say to the comments of others so the group stays on the topic. Also, be affirming whenever you can. This will encourage some of the more hesitant members of the group to participate.

3. Be careful not to dominate the discussion. We are sometimes so eager to share what we have learned that we do not leave opportunity for others to respond. By all means participate! But allow others to do so as well.

4. Expect God to teach you through the passage being discussed and through the other members of the group. Pray that you will have a profitable time together.

5. We recommend that groups follow a few basic guidelines, and that these guidelines be read at the beginning of each discussion session. The guidelines, which you may wish to adapt to your situation, are:

    a. Anything said in the group is considered confidential and will not be discussed outside the group unless specific permission is given to do so.

    b. We will provide time for each person present to talk if he or she feels comfortable doing so.

    c. We will talk about ourselves and our own situations, avoiding conversation about other people.

    d. We will listen attentively to each other.

    e. We will be very cautious about giving advice.

    f. We will pray for each other.

If you are the discussion leader, you will find additional suggestions and helpful ideas for each study in the leader's notes. These are found at the back of the guide.

Recovering from Bitterness

> Do not hate your brother in your heart. . . . Do not seek revenge
> or bear a grudge against one of your people, but love your neighbor
> as yourself. (Leviticus 19:17-18)
>
> Do not gloat when your enemy falls; when he stumbles, do not
> let your heart rejoice. (Proverbs 24:17)
>
> "Lord, how many times shall I forgive my brother when he sins
> against me? Up to seven times?" Jesus answered, "I tell you, not
> seven times, but seventy-seven times." (Matthew 18:21-22)

We know we should forgive. We know we should not be bitter.

There is, however, a significant problem. Forgiveness often gets
frustrated. It gets blocked and entangled. The process of forgiveness
often begins with the best of intentions, but then it somehow loses
its steam. The rage returns. The pain and the injustice overwhelm
us again. We find our hearts turning away from forgiveness toward
bitterness and desire for revenge.

Often with the return of bitterness, we experience discouragement
and shame. Our inability to forgive leads us to see ourselves as
spiritual failures.

Bitterness is an intense animosity toward another person that
erodes our peace of mind and robs us of joy. We need to recover from
bitterness because of what it does to us. We need to be healed of our
pain, freed from our rage and comforted in our grief so that we can

let go and move on in life. But once bitterness begins to grow, how do we get the process of forgiveness started again? It would be relatively easy if forgiveness were a simple matter of choice. Unfortunately, choosing to forgive is only a small part of what we need. The whole process of forgiveness requires much more than a willingness to forgive. C. S. Lewis put it this way:

> We find that the work of forgiveness has to be done over and over again. We forgive, we mortify our resentment; a week later some chain of thought carries us back to the original offence and we discover the old resentment blazing away as if nothing had been done about it at all. We need to forgive our brother seventy times seven not only for 490 offences but for one offence.[1]

Clearly, forgiveness is not some kind of magical incantation that we can use to make our pain disappear. Forgiveness is an emotionally costly struggle. It is, however, important because it is part of the struggle to live in solidarity with God and his kingdom. The struggle to forgive is the struggle to be like Jesus in whom we ourselves find forgiveness.

If you have ever tried to forgive someone and become frustrated because you were unable to do so, these studies are intended for you. Our prayer is that God will speak clearly to you and give you practical wisdom that you can apply to your struggle to forgive. We are convinced that it is possible to recover from bitterness, even though it is not an easy process. May God give you the courage and the wisdom you need to continue pursuing forgiveness.

May your roots sink deeply in the soil of God's love.

Dale and Juanita Ryan

---

[1]C. S. Lewis, *Reflections on the Psalms* (New York: Harcourt, Brace and World, Inc., 1958), p. 254.

1
Facing
the
Hurt

I was a very young child when my father began to abuse me. He was physically abusive to both my mom and to me. But he left home when I was nine. And I forgave him then—at least I honestly thought I forgave him. I can hardly remember him now. Why should it still matter? Why can't I just forget about it? Why do I still hate him?

Old anger and old pain. How we wish they would go away! How we wish that a simple choosing to forgive would put an end to it! But painful memories do not simply dissipate with time. Sometimes even after our best and most sincere efforts at forgiveness, we find that bitterness has found soil to grow in.

Bitterness often grows out of experiences which are so painful that the persons involved experience an initial state of shock in which they are unable to fully comprehend what has happened. This is a time of emotional numbness. In some ways, the shock can be helpful and important because it temporarily provides protection from the full emotional impact of a painful event. As the immediacy of the trauma passes, however, the emotions which were put on hold begin to return. The emotional Novocain gradually wears off, and the full emotional impact must be faced. It is at this point that the true struggle to forgive can begin.

Facing the return of the hurt, anger and loss can be a frightening experience. People may, often unknowingly, try to find ways to avoid or reject these feelings. Attempted detours around the emotional pain, however, make forgiveness more difficult. Recovery from bitterness cannot begin until a person begins to face the emotional pain of the past.

☐ **Personal Reflection** ————————————————————————————

1. What events in your past might be possible sources of bitterness for you?

2. What motivates you to want to struggle to forgive?

☐ **Bible Study**————————————————————————————————

Joseph was hated by his older brothers. This hatred was rooted in a history of family dysfunction. Joseph's mother was Jacob's favorite wife. And Joseph was Jacob's favorite son. Out of hatred for this family favorite, Joseph's brothers sold him into slavery. Joseph was taken away in chains to Egypt when he was a teen-ager. The events described in this text take place during a time of famine many years later. Joseph has risen from slavery to become an important political figure in Egypt.

When Jacob learned that there was grain in Egypt, he said to his sons, "Why do you just keep looking at each other?" He continued, "I have heard that there is grain in Egypt. Go down there and buy some for us, so that we may live and not die."

Then ten of Joseph's brothers went down to buy grain from Egypt. But Jacob did not send Benjamin, Joseph's brother, with the others, because he was afraid that harm might come to him. So Israel's sons were among those who went to buy grain, for the famine was in the land of Canaan also.

Now Joseph was the governor of the land, the one who sold grain to all its people. So when Joseph's brothers arrived, they bowed down to him with their faces to the ground. As soon as Joseph saw his brothers, he recognized them, but he pretended to be a stranger and spoke harshly to them. "Where do you come from?" he asked.

"From the land of Canaan," they replied, "to buy food."

Although Joseph recognized his brothers, they did not recognize him. Then he remembered his dreams about them and said to them, "You are spies! You have come to see where our land is unprotected."

"No, my lord," they answered. "Your servants have come to buy food. We are all the sons of one man. Your servants are honest men, not spies...."

They said to one another, "Surely we are being punished because of our brother. We saw how distressed he was when he pleaded with us for his life, but we would not listen; that's why this distress has come upon us."

Reuben replied, "Didn't I tell you not to sin against the boy? But you wouldn't listen! Now we must give an accounting for his blood." They did not realize that Joseph could understand them, since he was using an interpreter.

He turned away from them and began to weep, but then turned back and spoke to them again. He had Simeon taken from them and bound before their eyes. (Genesis 42:1-11, 21-24)

---

1. What insights did you gain during your time of personal reflection?

2. At the time of this story, Joseph was no longer the vulnerable teen-ager who had been hurt so deeply by his brothers. How did Joseph respond when he first saw his brothers?

3. What might Joseph have been thinking and feeling?

4. Not recognizing Joseph or realizing that he could understand their conversation, Joseph's brothers recounted to each other the terrible story of Joseph's enslavement. What did they say about it?

5. When his brothers recited this story, Joseph was vividly reminded of a terror-filled event from his past. What was the effect of that memory on Joseph?

6. What is frightening or difficult about remembering a past hurt?

7. Much later in the story, Joseph embraces his brothers and shows them mercy. He does not, however, embrace them at this meeting. Neither does he seem eager to forgive them. What is your response to this lack of forgiveness on Joseph's part?

8. What experiences have you had with trying to forgive prematurely?

9. What might give you the courage to face past hurts?

☐ **Prayer** ————————————————————————————————

What would you like to say to God about past hurts which you have experienced?

2
Feeling
Anger

When we recognize that we have been hurt and we allow ourselves to feel the hurt, we often begin to experience anger.

For most of us, anger is not a comfortable emotion. For some of us, it is a terrifying emotion. We know the damage that anger can do. We know the pain it can cause. We fear our own capacity for evil when we are angry. We recognize our desire for revenge. We know that we have been hurt, and we know that anger feeds our longing to hurt back.

Anger is, however, a common experience in the struggle to forgive. Avoiding anger will not make it go away, but can instead allow it to grow into bitterness. Feeling anger and expressing it honestly to God and to others makes it possible for us to continue growing toward forgiveness.

There are, of course, both helpful and unhelpful things we can do with our anger. Denying, avoiding, minimizing and blaming others for it are just a few of the many unhelpful ways of responding to anger. The text for this study suggests that one helpful thing to do with anger is to let it motivate us to pray honestly and passionately.

Moving from nice, safe, respectable prayers toward prayers which express our true feelings to God can be enormously helpful in the struggle to forgive.

☐ **Personal Reflection** ——————————————————————

1. What do you usually do when you are angry with someone who is important to you?

2. What are your thoughts and feelings about yourself when you are angry?

3. What past event(s) still arouse feelings of anger within you?

☐ Bible Study———————————————————————————

O God, whom I praise,
    do not remain silent,
for wicked and deceitful men
have opened their mouths against me;
    they have spoken against me with lying tongues.
With words of hatred they surround me;
    they attack me without cause.
In return for my friendship they accuse me,
    but I am a man of prayer.
They repay me evil for good,
    and hatred for my friendship.

Appoint an evil man to oppose him;
    let an accuser stand at his right hand.
When he is tried, let him be found guilty,
    and may his prayers condemn him.
May his days be few;
    may another take his place of leadership.
May his children be fatherless
    and his wife a widow.
May his children be wandering beggars;
    may they be driven from their ruined homes.
May a creditor seize all he has;
    may strangers plunder the fruits of his labor.
May no one extend kindness to him
    or take pity on his fatherless children
May his descendants be cut off,
    their names blotted out from the next generation.

For I am poor and needy,
    and my heart is wounded within me.
I fade away like an evening shadow;

I am shaken off like a locust.
My knees give way from fasting;
    my body is thin and gaunt.
I am an object of scorn to my accusers;
    when they see me, they shake their heads.

Help me, O LORD my God;
    save me in accordance with your love.
Let them know that it is your hand,
    that you, O LORD, have done it.
They may curse, but you will bless;
    when they attack they will be put to shame,
    but your servant will rejoice.
My accusers will be clothed with disgrace
    and wrapped in shame as in a cloak.

With my mouth I will greatly extol the LORD;
    in the great throng I will praise him.
For he stands at the right hand of the needy one,
    to save his life from those who condemn him.
    (Psalm 109:1-13, 22-31)

---

1. What insights did you gain during your time of personal reflection?

2. To what painful experiences is the author reacting?

3. The speaker is particularly outraged at the injustice of his accusers. "They repay me evil for good, and hatred for my friendship." How does this add to his sense of rage?

4. What does the author ask God to do to his enemies?

5. What thoughts and feelings do you have as you read the angry cry for revenge?

6. The author describes the effects which the painful events have had on him. Which of these effects have you experienced?

7. How would expressing your anger to God be helpful to you?

8. God is described at the end as being on the side of the "needy" and "condemned." How could seeing God in this way be a practical help to you when you are angry?

9. How can other people be helpful to you in your struggle with anger?

☐ **Prayer** _____

What anger do you want to express to God today?

3
Grieving

Facing the hurt and experiencing anger help us to identify and feel what has happened to us. Another part of the process of moving out of our emotional numbness is allowing ourselves to grieve over the losses we have experienced.

When we experience an event or series of events which are hurtful, we experience losses. These are not necessarily the loss of possessions or things. The losses might include losses of self-esteem, identity, expectations, or a sense of security and belonging. All of these losses may cause us to grieve.

Grieving is the process of identifying and experiencing these losses. It is not an easy experience. It can be exhausting physically, emotionally and spiritually. Grieving is full of questions. When we grieve, we ask ourselves such questions as: "What is wrong with me?" "Am I exaggerating?" "Am I just being childish?" We also ask questions of God: "Where were you?" "Why did you let this happen?" "Why this injustice?"

Although grief is difficult, it is a normal response to any loss, and it is an important step toward forgiveness. It is also an experience which is potentially enriching. "Blessed are those who grieve," Jesus said, "for they will be comforted."

☐ **Personal Reflection** _____

1. What losses have you experienced that make it difficult to forgive those who have harmed you?

2. Write a short prayer to God which describes these losses. Ask God to help you to grieve over these losses in ways that cause you to grow.

☐ **Bible Study** _____

O LORD, do not rebuke me in your anger
    or discipline me in your wrath.
Be merciful to me, LORD, for I am faint;
    O Lord, heal me, for my bones are in agony.
My soul is in anguish.
    How long, O LORD, how long?

Turn, O LORD, and deliver me;
    save me because of your unfailing love.
No one remembers you when he is dead.
    Who praises you from the grave?

I am worn out from groaning;
    all night long I flood my bed with weeping
    and drench my couch with tears.
My eyes grow weak with sorrow;
    they fail because of all my foes.
Away from me, all you who do evil,
    for the LORD has heard my weeping.
The LORD has heard my cry for mercy;
    the LORD accepts my prayer.
All my enemies will be ashamed and dismayed;
    they will turn back in sudden disgrace. (Psalm 6)

---

1. What insights did you gain during your time of personal reflection?

2. What information does the author give about the cause of his grief?

3. How do the physical manifestations of grief described compare with what you have experienced as you struggle to forgive?

4. How do the emotional realities described compare with what you have experienced as you struggle to forgive?

5. This prayer begins with an expression of anxiety about God. The author seems to be afraid that God might judge him rather than help him as he grieves. What is it about grief that makes God seem so far away?

6. The author also expresses some frustration about God's slow response to his situation. He says, "How long, O LORD, how long?" What is it about the experience of grief that makes it seem so long?

7. This prayer confirms what we all know to be true: Grief is an unpleasant physical, emotional and spiritual experience. What value is there in allowing ourselves to grieve when it is so unpleasant?

8. By the end of his prayer, the author seems less anxious about God and more confident of his love. He says that God has heard him and accepted him. How might it help you in your struggle to forgive to know that God accepts your weeping?

9. What would give you the courage to grieve over the losses which have led to your bitterness?

☐ **Prayer** _____

What would you like to ask of the God who hears your weeping?

4
Letting
Go

The only thing I have to remind me that I really matter in all of this is my anger and my depression. I feel like I've lost everything else. I don't want to lose these too.

When we have experienced significant losses, it is often hard to let go of anything. We find ourselves holding on tenaciously. To let go would be to give in, to make it O.K., to be at risk of getting hurt again. And we can't let that happen.

An important turning point in the process of forgiveness comes when we can begin to explore the possibility of letting go. Finding ways to let go that do not set us up for revictimization will take some thoughtful searching, but it is possible to let go in healthy, growth-producing ways. We can let go of unrealistic expectations of ourselves and of others. We can let go of feelings of responsibility for other people's behavior. And we can let go of revenge.

It is important to remember that we may experience many cycles of holding on and letting go during our struggle to forgive. Forgiveness is not something to "do and be done with," but an ongoing process of opening our hurts to God's healing love.

☐ Personal Reflection ————————————————————

1. What pain, anger or bitterness would you like to be able to give to God?

2. What makes it difficult for you to let go?

☐ Bible Study——————————————————————

If it is possible, as far as it depends on you, live at peace with everyone. Do not take revenge, my friends, but leave room for God's wrath, for it is written: "It is mine to avenge; I will repay," says the Lord. On the contrary:
   "If your enemy is hungry, feed him; if he is thirsty, give him something to drink. In doing this, you will heap burning coals on his head."
Do not be overcome by evil, but overcome evil with good. (Romans 12:18-21)

1. What insights did you gain during your time of personal reflection?

2. The passage teaches us not to be overcome by evil. What does it mean to be overcome by evil?

3. "Living at peace" stands in sharp contrast to "being overcome by evil." The phrase "if possible" implies that we should be realistic about the process of making peace. What are some of the unrealistic ideas about living at peace that you may need to let go of?

4. The phrase "as far as it depends on you" suggests that living at peace is not entirely under our control. We need to let go of inappropriate feelings of responsibility for other people's behavior. How can remembering this be helpful in your journey toward forgiveness?

5. In addition to letting go of unrealistic expectations and of our attempts to control other people, we need to let go of our desire for revenge. What reason does the text give for letting go of revenge?

6. How would it help you in your struggle to forgive to let go of the desire for revenge?

7. The revolutionary element in this text is the instruction to "overcome evil with good." How could acts of kindness help you in your struggle to forgive?

8. If doing acts of kindness is a way of pretending that we have not been hurt, these acts are not likely to help us in our recovery. What is the difference between "overcoming evil with good" and pretending everything is fine?

9. Write one or two sentences on a piece of paper about a hurt which has been difficult for you to forgive. Seal the hurt in an envelope. Offer it to God with this prayer: "I give this to you. I want to let go of my desire for revenge, my unrealistic expectations and my attempts to fix this. If revenge is needed, I leave it to you. I open myself to doing good. Help me to overcome this evil with good." Dramatize your letting go by burning the envelope or throwing it away.

What thoughts and feelings did you have during this exercise?

☐ **Prayer** _____

How would you like God to help you to let go?

5
Choosing Growth

"Struggle brings opportunities for growth." *Unfortunately, this state*-ment could easily qualify for the list of "most frequently trivialized truths of all time." Nothing is less helpful in the struggle to forgive than to have people who seem relentlessly cheerful remind you of all the wonderful opportunities for growth they see in your situation. It is just another attempt to avoid the painful realities of the recovery process.

Most of us find it difficult to welcome growth that comes during the struggle to forgive. It feels somehow like giving in or like some kind of verbal gymnastics that allows evil to masquerade as good. We don't buy it. No "building character" can compensate for evil. It doesn't make sense.

There is, however, a time for growth. Not before the pain. Not instead of the pain. But the time to welcome growth does come.

Christians believe that the opportunity for growth will come because God is at work in the tragedies and has not abandoned us to evil. God has not hidden himself from our suffering. He has not minimized, denied or avoided. He has faced all the evil with us and is prepared to be with us when it is time to grow.

□ **Personal Reflection** _____

1. What good has come (or could come) from your struggle to forgive?

2. What factors made (or could make) this growth possible?

□ **Bible Study**_____

Grace and peace be yours in abundance through the knowledge of God and of Jesus our Lord.

His divine power has given us everything we need for life and godliness through our knowledge of him who called us by his own glory and goodness. Through these he has given us his very great and precious promises, so that through them you may participate in the divine nature and escape the corruption in the world caused by evil desires.

For this very reason, make every effort to add to your faith goodness; and to goodness, knowledge; and to knowledge, self-control; and to self-control, perseverance; and to perseverance, godliness; and to godliness, brotherly kindness; and to brotherly kindness, love. For if you possess these qualities in increasing measure, they will keep you from being ineffective and unproductive in your knowledge of our Lord Jesus Christ. (2 Peter 1:2-8)

---

1. What insights did you gain during your time of personal reflection?

2. This is taken from a letter written by Peter, a leader in the early church, to the people he ministered to. What does Peter say about the resources God makes available to us?

3. How might these resources contribute to your growth while you are struggling to forgive?

4. Peter's encouragement that we should possess certain "qualities in increasing measure" implies that growth is a process. What has the process of growth been like for you as you have struggled to forgive?

5. Which of the seven character qualities listed by Peter do you see developing in yourself?

6. What other character qualities would you like to grow toward?

7. Peter recognizes that growth requires effort. What efforts have helped you grow as you have struggled to forgive?

8. What additional efforts might help you to continue in the process of growth?

☐ **Prayer** ————————————————————————

In what areas would you like God to help you grow?

6
Finding Purpose

"I didn't make this mess. Why should I have to be the one to clean it up?"

Our kids ask that question all the time. It's a pretty good question. It's also fair to wonder, "Why should I have to do all the hard work that goes into forgiveness when I'm not the one who started this?" It doesn't make sense. And the senselessness of it can make it much harder for us to stay committed to the process. It is especially difficult if we see our struggle to forgive as an isolated, meaningless struggle. We need some context for this struggle that gives it meaning.

Christians have always believed that the struggle to forgive is a participation in God's redemptive purposes. It is purposeful because it is a struggle that God is committed to. As the text for this study will suggest, to struggle toward forgiveness is to struggle to be like Jesus.

Jesus knows that forgiveness is costly. Providing forgiveness for our sins cost him his life. When Jesus faced the cross, his struggle was intense. Being like Jesus doesn't mean that forgiveness will come easy for us. We do well to encourage each other by remembering that struggle is not a sign of spiritual failure. God does not ask us to forgive quickly and easily. God knows personally that forgiveness is costly.

☐ Personal Reflection _____

1. Many people experience shame when they are told that we should follow Jesus' example in forgiveness. How do *you* respond to the idea of following Jesus' example?

2. What has discouraged you in your struggle to forgive?

3. What has encouraged you in your struggle to forgive?

☐ Bible Study _____

Then Jesus went with his disciples to a place called Gethsemane, and he said to them, "Sit here while I go over there and pray." He took Peter and the two sons of Zebedee along with him, and he began to be sorrowful and troubled. Then he said to them, "My soul is overwhelmed with sorrow to the point of death. Stay here and keep watch with me."

Going a little farther, he fell with his face to the ground and prayed, "My Father, if it is possible, may this cup be taken from me. Yet not as I will, but as you will."

Then he returned to his disciples and found them sleeping. "Could you men not keep watch with me for one hour?" he asked Peter. "Watch and pray so that you will not fall into temptation. The spirit is willing, but the body is weak."

He went away a second time and prayed, "My Father, if it is not possible for this cup to be taken away unless I drink it, may your will be done."

When he came back, he again found them sleeping, because their eyes were heavy. So he left them and went away once more and prayed the third time, saying the same thing.

Then he returned to the disciples and said to them, "Are you still sleeping and resting? Look, the hour is near, and the Son of Man is betrayed into the hands of sinners. Rise, let us go! Here comes my betrayer!" (Matthew 26:36-46)

When they came to the place called the Skull, there they crucified him, along with the criminals—one on his right, the other on his left. Jesus said, "Father, forgive them, for they do not know what they are doing." (Luke 23:33-34)

---

1. What insights did you gain during your time of personal reflection?

2. This account shows Jesus praying to God over his anticipated death on the cross. We can see that bearing the cost of forgiveness was not easy for Jesus. How is Jesus' struggle described?

3. Jesus prayed three times to be spared the suffering that forgiveness would cost him. How does knowing that Jesus prayed this way help you to continue your struggle to forgive?

4. How does Jesus' struggle with forgiveness compare to your own experience?

5. Jesus asked his closest friends to be with him while he grieved over the cost of forgiveness. How do you think his friends could have been helpful to Jesus?

6. How could friends be helpful to you in your struggle to forgive?

7. Jesus brings forgiveness to completion on the cross by asking God to forgive those who crucified him. How does the possibility of being able to come to this point encourage you to continue with the process?

8. The struggle to forgive is the struggle to be like Jesus. How might this perspective help you to continue your struggle to forgive?

9. Spend a few minutes visualizing the scene of Jesus on the cross. Picture the person(s) you struggle to forgive in the crowd around the cross. Listen to Jesus say "Father, forgive them." Allow yourself to see God forgiving the people who have harmed you.

What thoughts and feelings do you have in response to this meditation?

☐ **Prayer** ———————————————————————

What help do you need from God in your struggle to be like Jesus?

Leáder's Notes

You may be experiencing a variety of feelings as you anticipate leading a group using a Life Recovery Guide. You may feel inadequate and afraid of what will happen. If this is the case, know you are in good company. Many of the kings, prophets and apostles in the Bible felt inadequate and afraid. Many other small group leaders share the experience of fear as well.

Your willingness to lead, however, is a gift to the other group members. It might help if you tell them about your feelings and ask them to pray for you. Keep in mind that the other group members share the responsibility for the group. And realize that it is God's work to bring insight, comfort, healing and recovery to group members. Your role is simply to provide guidance for the discussion. The suggestions listed below will help you to provide that guidance.

Using the Life Recovery Guide Series
This Life Recovery Guide is one in a series of eight guides. The series was designed to be a flexible tool that can be used in various combinations by individuals and groups—such as support groups, Bible studies and Sunday-school classes. Each guide contains six studies. If all eight guides are used, they can provide a year-long curriculum series. Or if the guides are used in pairs, they can provide studies for a quarter (twelve weeks).

We want to emphasize that all of the guides in this series are designed to be useful to anyone. Each guide has a specific focus, but all are written with a general audience in mind. Additionally, the workbook format allows for personal interaction with biblical truths, making the guides adaptable to each individual's unique journey in recovery.

The four guides which all individuals and groups should find they can most easily relate to are *Recovery from Distorted Images of God, Recovery from Loss, Recovery from Bitterness* and *Recovery from Shame.* All of us need to replace our distorted images of God with biblically accurate images. All of us experience losses, disappointments and disillusionment in life, as well as loss through death or illness. We all have life experiences and relationships which lead to bitterness and which make forgiveness difficult. And we all experience shame and its debilitating consequences.

The four other guides are *Recovery from Codependency, Recovery from Family Dysfunctions, Recovery from Abuse* and *Recovery from Addictions.* Although these guides have a more specific focus, they address issues of very general concern both within the Christian community and in our culture as a whole. The biblical resources will be helpful to your recovery even if you do not share the specific concerns which these guides address.

Individuals who are working on a specific life issue and groups with a shared focus may want to begin with the guide which relates most directly to their concerns. Survivors of abuse, for example, may want to work through *Recovery from Abuse* and follow it with *Recovery from Shame.* Adult children from dysfunctional families may want to begin with *Recovery from Family Dysfunctions* and then use *Recovery from Distorted Images of God.* And those who struggle with addictive patterns may want to begin with *Recovery from Addictions* and then use *Recovery from Codependency.*

There are many other possibilities for study combinations. The short descriptions of each guide on the last page, as well as the information on the back of each guide will help you to further decide which guides will be most helpful to your recovery.

Preparing to Lead

1. Develop realistic expectations of yourself as a small group leader. Do not feel that you have to "have it all together." Rather, commit yourself to an ongoing discipline of honesty about your own needs. As you grow in honesty about your own needs, you will grow as well in your capacity for compassion, gentleness and patience with yourself and with others. As a leader, you can encourage an atmosphere of honesty by being honest about yourself.

2. Pray. Pray for yourself and your own recovery. Pray for the group members. Invite the Holy Spirit to be present as you prepare and as you meet.

3. Read the study several times.

4. Take your time to thoughtfully work through each question, writing out your answers.

5. After completing your personal study, read through the leader's notes for the study you are leading. These notes are designed to help you in several ways. First, they tell you the purpose the authors had in mind while writing the study. Take time to think through how the questions work together to accomplish that purpose. Second, the notes provide you with additional background information or comments on some of the questions. This information can be useful if people have difficulty understanding or answering a question. Third, the leader's notes can alert you to potential problems you may encounter during the study.

6. If you wish to remind yourself during the group discussion of anything mentioned in the leader's notes, make a note to yourself below that question in your study guide.

Leading the Study

1. Begin on time. You may want to open in prayer, or have a group member do so.

2. Be sure everyone has a study guide. Decide as a group if you want people to do the study on their own ahead of time. If your time together is limited, it will be helpful for people to prepare in advance.

3. At the beginning of your first time together, explain that these studies are meant to be discussions, not lectures. Encourage the members of the group to participate. However, do not put pressure on those who may be hesitant to speak during the first few sessions. Clearly state that people do not need to share anything they do not feel safe sharing. Remind people that it will take time to trust each other.

4. Read aloud the group guidelines listed in the front of the guide. These commitments are important in creating a safe place for people to talk and trust and feel.

5. The covers of the Life Recovery Guides are designed to incorporate both symbols of the past and hope for the future. During your first meeting, allow the group to describe what they see in the cover and respond to it.

6. Read aloud the introductory paragraphs at the beginning of the discussion for the day. This will orient the group to the passage being studied.

7. The personal reflection questions are designed to help group members focus on some aspect of their experience. Hopefully, they will help group members to be more aware of the frame of reference and life experience which they bring to the study. The personal reflection section can be done prior to the group meeting or as the first part of the meeting. If the group does not prepare in advance, approximately ten minutes will be needed for individuals to consider these questions.

The personal reflection questions are not designed to be used directly for group discussion. Rather, the first question in the Bible study section is intended to give group members an opportunity to reveal what they feel safe sharing from their time of personal reflection.

8. Read the passage aloud. You may choose to do this yourself, or prior to the study you might ask someone else to read.

9. As you begin to ask the questions in the guide, keep several things in mind. First, the questions are designed to be used just as they are written. If you wish, you may simply read them aloud to the group. Or you may prefer to express them in your own words. However, unnecessary rewording of the questions is not recommended.

Second, the questions are intended to guide the group toward understanding and applying the main idea of the study. You will find the purpose of each study described in the leader's notes. You should try to understand how the study questions and the biblical text work together to lead the group in that direction.

There may be times when it is appropriate to deviate from the study guide. For example, a question may have already been answered. If so, move on to the next question. Or someone may raise an important question not covered in the guide. Take time to discuss it! The important thing is to use discretion. There may be many routes you can travel to reach the goal of the study. But the easiest route is usually the one we have suggested.

10. Don't be afraid of silence. People need time to think about the question before formulating their answers.

11. Draw out a variety of responses from the group. Ask, "Who else has some thoughts about this?" or "How did some of the rest of you respond?" until several people have given answers to the question.

12. Acknowledge all contributions. Try to be affirming whenever possible. Never reject an answer. If it seems clearly wrong to you, ask, "Which part of the text led you to that conclusion?" or "What do the rest of you think?"

13. Realize that not every answer will be addressed to you, even though this will probably happen at first. As group members become more at ease, they will begin to interact more effectively with each other. This is a sign of a healthy discussion.

14. Don't be afraid of controversy. It can be very stimulating. Differences can enrich our lives. If you don't resolve an issue completely, don't be frustrated. Move on and keep it in mind for later. A subsequent study may resolve the problem. Or, the issue may not be resolved—not all questions have answers!

15. Stick to the passage under consideration. It should be the source for answering the questions. Discourage the group from unnecessary cross-referencing. Likewise, stick to the subject and avoid going off on tangents.

16. Periodically summarize what the group has said about the topic. This helps to draw together the various ideas mentioned and gives continuity to the study. But be careful not to use summary statements as an opportunity to give a sermon!

17. During the discussion, feel free to share your own responses. Your honesty about your own recovery can set a tone for the group to feel safe in sharing. Be careful not to dominate the time, but do allow time for your own needs as a group member.

18. Each study ends with a time for prayer. There are several ways to handle this time in a group. The person who leads each study could lead the group in a prayer or you could allow time for group participation. Remember that some members of your group may feel uncomfortable about participating in public prayer. It might be helpful to discuss this with the group during your first meeting and to reach some agreement about how to proceed.

19. Realize that trust in a group grows over time. During the first couple meetings, people will be assessing how safe they will feel in the group. Do not be discouraged if people share only superficially at first. The level of trust will grow slowly but steadily.

Listening to Emotional Pain

Life Recovery Guides are designed to take seriously the pain and struggle that is part of life. People will experience a variety of emotions during these studies. Your role as group leader is not to act as a professional counselor. Instead it is to be a friend who listens to emotional pain. Listening is a gift you can give to hurting people. For many, it is not an easy gift to give. The following suggestions can help you listen more effectively to people in emotional pain.

1. Remember that you are not responsible to take the pain away. People in helping relationships often feel that they are being asked to make the other person feel better. This is usually related to the helper's own patterns of not being comfortable with painful feelings.

2. Not only are you not responsible to take the pain away, one of the things people need most is an opportunity to face and to experience the pain in their lives. They have usually spent years denying their pain and running from it. Healing can come when we are able to face our pain in the presence of someone who cares about us. Rather than trying to take the pain away, commit yourself to listening attentively as it is expressed.

3. Realize that some group members may not feel comfortable with expressions of sadness or anger. You may want to acknowledge that such emotions are uncomfortable, but remind the group that part of recovery is to learn to feel and to allow others to feel.

4. Be very cautious about giving answers and advice. Advice and answers may make you feel better or feel competent, but they may also minimize people's problems and their painful feelings. Simple solutions rarely work, and they can easily communicate "You should be better now" or "You shouldn't really be talking about this."

5. Be sure to communicate direct affirmation any time people talk about their painful emotions. It takes courage to talk about our pain because it creates anxiety for us. It is a great gift to be trusted by those who are struggling.

The following notes refer to the questions in the Bible study portion of each study:

Study 1. Facing the Hurt. Genesis 42:1-11; 21-24.
Purpose: To identify the hurts which have led to bitterness.
Question 2. Joseph pretended to be a stranger and spoke harshly, accusingly to them. He was not nice.
Question 3. Joseph must have been thinking "These are the people

who hated me, who betrayed me, who wanted to kill me." He might have felt the return of anger and fear and sorrow.

Question 4. The brothers recount rather graphically "how distressed young Joseph was, how he pleaded for his life." See Genesis 37:12-28 if you want to read the account of Joseph being sold. It must have been a terrible scene. He was ripped away from his family, given to people who could use him any way they wanted. Joseph probably screamed and yelled and pleaded with his brothers, but they sold him anyway.

Question 5. It caused him pain. He wept. He felt the hurt of what had happened to him. If you read further in Joseph's story, you will find that he wept on several occasions as he continued to experience this painful memory.

Question 6. One of the most disconcerting things about recovery from bitterness is the longevity of our painful memories. We want to believe that things which happened a decade ago are long gone. We have many sayings which reinforce our desire to minimize the effect of old pain (for example, "Let bygones be bygones," "That's just water under the bridge" or "What's done is done"). But painful emotions do not just go away as time passes. Old pain, long neglected, may re-emerge with frightening immediacy when provoked by an event such as the one Joseph experienced.

Question 7. A common response might be to think: "Shouldn't Joseph be better by now? He's had all these years! Things have worked out for good—he is in a position to rescue his family from the famine." The main issue to discuss here is: Are painful emotions a problem which forgiveness solves, or are painful emotions a necessary stage in the process which leads to forgiveness? If the former is true, then the sooner Joseph "gets over" his emotional pain the better. If the latter is true, then the sooner Joseph allows himself to experience his painful emotions, the more likely that true forgiveness will emerge.

Question 8. People may be able to be more understanding of Joseph and his painful emotions than they are of their own. It's one thing to appreciate Joseph's story, it's another to give oneself permission to experience pain over events that happened a long time ago. Encourage group members to explore their desires to get it over with as soon as possible.

Question 9. Courage comes from (1) relationships in which you experience acceptance and accountability, (2) seeing other people deal with their painful memories, (3) knowing that God wants you to experience freedom from the bondage of painful memories, and (4) the active participation of the Holy Spirit.

Study 2. Feeling Anger. Psalm 109:1-13, 22-31.

Purpose: To encourage honest expression of anger to God in prayer.

Question 2. The author is apparently reacting to a false accusation. His response to this event will be familiar to people who have experienced any trauma that led to bitterness.

Question 3. It is very painful to be betrayed by someone you have trusted—for example, the child who seeks to please his or her parents and receives abuse in return, the spouse who is abandoned for another, the parents whose love is rejected.

Question 4. The desire for vengeance is unmistakable. Modern readers may find it particularly offensive that the author's anger leads to a desire for evil to happen to his enemy's children. It may make it more intelligible, though certainly no less offensive, to remember that individualism was foreign to the author's tribal culture. Individual identities were inseparable from their identities as members of a multi-generational household. People in the author's culture were not distinct from their ancestors or their descendants—to curse one was to curse them all.

The point to focus on here is not whether the author's desires were appropriate. (They clearly are not.) The important point is that we will experience these kinds of feelings and desires and God is accustomed to listening to prayers of this kind.

Question 5. Ambivalence about the vindictiveness is unavoidable. For some people the words of the author may be shocking and frightening. For others it may come as a relief to know that the author experienced rage and a desire for revenge and was able to be passionately honest with God about them. Consider C. S. Lewis's comment on prayers of this kind:

> The hatred is there—festering, gloating, undisguised—and also we should be wicked if we in any way condoned or approved it, or (worse still) used it to justify similar passions in ourselves. We can still see, in the worst of their maledictions, how these old poets were, in a sense, near to God. Though hideously distorted by the human instrument, something of the Divine voice can be heard in these passages. Not, of course, that God looks upon their enemies as they do: He "desireth not the death of a sinner." But doubtless He has for the sin of those enemies just the implacable hostility which the poets express." (C. S. Lewis, *Reflections on the Psalms* [New York: Harcourt, Brace and World, 1958], pp. 22, 32)

Question 7. We covet the author's ability to name his emotions and share them so freely with God. What better thing to do with all the hopelessly entangled emotions than to bring them out into the open in the presence of God. After listening to the author and to generations of the faithful who have used the psalms as a guide to prayer, God is not likely to be shocked by anything we have to say!

Question 8. It is possible that this study will end without the kind of resolution that leaders usually enjoy. We would feel a lot better if our anger could somehow be resolved today. But anger that has been nurtured or ignored for years will not resolve in a single discussion. Remind your group that acknowledging anger is an important part of the struggle to forgive. It is not the whole process, but it is an important part. Encourage your group to have reasonable expectations about recovery.

Question 9. We can help each other by listening, giving permission for anger, not being shocked, realizing that talking about it will take some of the power out of it, and encouraging each other in recovery.

Study 3. Grieving. Psalm 6.

Purpose: To acknowledge the losses which have contributed to bitterness.

Question 2. Not much information is given except that he is grieving over a hurt caused by an "enemy." An important point to emphasize is that grief is not just a way of coming to terms with the death of someone you love but is also an important part of the struggle to forgive someone who has hurt you.

Question 3. The physical symptoms listed by the author are common in grief experiences: groaning, sleeplessness, weakness, faintness and exhaustion.

Question 4. The emotional symptoms included here are agony, anguish and weeping.

Question 5. People who experience grief as they struggle to forgive often shame themselves for not being able to forgive or to let go of their painful emotions. They think: "I shouldn't be feeling this sad and angry. There must be something wrong with me. God is going to reject me because of it."

Question 6. Grief almost always feels like an eternity. Sadness doesn't feel like it's going anywhere. Grief seems so unproductive. People often report feeling that if they started to cry they might never be able to stop. Frustration about God's responsiveness to our struggles and a longing for him to participate more actively in our lives is a remarkably common biblical theme. God understands this frustration. He also longs for a closer relationship with us (see, for example, Matthew 23:37; Isaiah 30:18).

Question 7. Grieving is part of the process of facing what is real, part of the necessary preparations for forgiveness.

Study 4. Letting Go. Romans 12:18-21.

Purpose: To learn to let go in ways that allow forgiveness.

Question 2. To be overcome by evil means that the evil done to us has taken control of our lives. If we hang on to our bitterness, evil will have overcome us. It is important to emphasize that experiencing the painful emotions which are part of the process of forgiveness is not "being overcome." Feeling what you feel is a sign that the struggle to forgive is continuing. The pain has not "overcome" you if the struggle goes on.

Question 3. The phrase "if possible" suggests the importance of realistic expectations about the process. Peace is not always possible. Forgiveness does not always lead to reconciliation because reconciliation requires both parties to be changed. Unrealistic expectations might include: "I should avoid conflict at any cost" or "It's entirely up to me to make sure everyone is happy."

Question 4. You can't control an alcoholic's drinking. You can't control someone else's behavior. You can't get the other person to say "I'm sorry." You can't force someone into reconciliation. The phrase "as far as it depends on you" emphasizes that we are not responsible to change the other person. We are responsible for our own thoughts and behaviors, but we have no helpful role in fixing the other person.

Question 5. Fundamentally, revenge is not our responsibility. Our revenge doesn't give God room to fulfill his responsibility. It may be important to emphasize that God's wrath is not like the unpredictable, irrational, unjust malice that so many people have experienced. To "leave room for God's wrath" is to leave room for justice!

It might be helpful to note that there are several steps to letting go of revenge. Letting go of revengeful behaviors probably will come before letting go of the desire for revenge. Encourage the group to take the next step and to be patient with themselves in the struggle to let go.

Question 6. Revenge is an attempt to even the score. It is never possible to "get even." Engaging in revenge means engaging in violent thoughts, words and actions. All such violence will hurt us. It may even destroy us. Letting go of revenge frees you up to experience peace—the painful events of the past are turned over to God. This does not mean that we abandon our desire for justice. Rather it means that we trust God, who is wiser than we are, to be the agent of justice.

Question 7. One of the fears we have when we have been hurt is that revenge will cause us to become like the person who has hurt us—abuse can lead to more abuse. An act of kindness to someone who has hurt you can reassure you that you are not caught in a vicious cycle. Abuse does not need to lead to more abuse. Violence does not need to lead to more violence.

Another common fear is that we will never recover. A tangible act of kindness can be a powerful reminder that we do not need to be consumed by this pain.

This text is a quote from Proverbs 25:21-22. The meaning of the expression "heap burning coals on his head" is uncertain. It could refer to a punishment. If so, the text means that "if we displace revenge with love, God will be able to bring about justice." Others think it refers to an Egyptian expiation ritual in which people held bowls of burning coals above their heads as a sign of repentance. If the latter is correct, then the sense of the passage is that "displacing revenge with acts of love may lead to the repentance of an enemy."

Question 8. This text does not minimize the pain caused by evil; it does not say "pretend" or "let go" of your painful emotions. It says to let go of unrealistic expectations, of taking inappropriate responsibility for others and of revenge.

"Being nice" is usually a dysfunctional way of trying to get someone else to change. The text is not specific about what kinds of behaviors constitute doing "good," beyond responding to basic needs (hunger and thirst). The principle is no doubt intended to have a broad application. The text does not say, however, "Be so good that the person changes" (see note to question 4).

Question 9. This can be a particularly powerful group activity. The envelopes can be burned or destroyed in other ways. The drama is:

"I let go of this. I make room for God's wrath. I open myself to doing good rather than evil."

Study 5. Choosing Growth. 2 Peter 1:2-8.

Purpose: To prepare ourselves to accept growth as part of the struggle to forgive.

Question 2. The text suggests that God can give us grace and peace in abundance, everything we need for a life of godliness, very great and precious promises and "participation" in the divine nature. These are very large concepts. It might be helpful to have group members reflect on what they mean to them.

Question 3. We have a powerful God on our side. He is not working against us, but for us. And his resources are unlimited. Knowing this can help us to realize that we are not alone in our struggle to forgive and can give us solid reason for hope in moments of discouragement.

Question 5. Abandoning the struggle to forgive often leads to bitterness. Continuing the struggle often leads to personal growth. People may be hesitant to acknowledge the good things God is doing in their lives. But it is important to help each other acknowledge our growth. Group members may be able to affirm ways in which they have seen each other grow.

Question 6. Peter talks about growth as having some degree of intentionality even though it is not entirely under our control. It is possible to identify goals for personal growth and to work toward them.

Question 7. Growth is a process that requires commitment and effort. It is hard work to struggle to forgive. It is hard work to grow. Some people may assume that Peter's encouragement that we participate actively in our own growth may reflect unrealistic expectations. Peter is not saying, "If only you worked harder, you would be further along in recovery, or if only you put more effort into it, you could forgive." Some people may beat up on themselves by deciding they haven't worked long enough or hard enough or consistently enough. The problem is that this "not enough" language discourages us and causes us to discount the good things that God is doing in our lives. It is important that we look at the efforts we have made and allow ourselves to celebrate them and to give thanks to God for them.

Question 8. "Efforts" that contribute to growth may include the disciplines of prayer and Bible study. Efforts at honesty about ourselves, efforts toward deeper intimacy in friendships, efforts to be more compassionate with ourselves and others are a few other examples of efforts that contribute to spiritual growth. Efforts may also include the hard work of recovery in therapy or in a support group setting.

Study 6. Finding Purpose. Matthew 26:36-46; Luke 23:33-34.
Purpose: To see the connection between the struggle to forgive, and God's redemptive purposes in Christ.

Question 2. Many people think that "being like Jesus" means being able to forgive easily, quickly, without emotional suffering. This story suggests that Jesus' struggle to provide us with forgiveness was extremely painful. He was "overwhelmed with sorrow to the point of death." When we struggle to forgive, we are being like Jesus.

Question 3. It is not because we are "bad" that we struggle, and it does not mean we are failures as Christians. This truth can give us courage and hope in the midst of the struggle.

Question 5. Friends can decrease the sense of isolation people feel when they are experiencing the painful emotions of struggling for forgiveness. We ask "Who else really understands this?" In our deepest struggles we often think we should be able to manage by ourselves. This has never been God's intention. Jesus asked for companionship in suffering. We would do well to be like him.

Question 7. Often the process of forgiveness must be repeated more than once. Sometimes it feels like the process goes on and on. But you will not be this angry and full of grief forever. There is a completion to the process of forgiveness. If you are not at the end today, that's probably not surprising. But there is an end—and that's good news.

Christians believe that all hope for relationship with God depends on God's capacity for forgiveness. We have sinned. If God can't genuinely forgive, then we are without hope. It is critically important for us that God's forgiveness be real, full, complete, genuine forgiveness.

Some people wonder: What if God should minimize, avoid or pretend about the suffering we have caused him? What if he should forgive prematurely? What if God's forgiveness leaves behind unaddressed pain in which bitterness can grow? Christians believe that Christ's death demonstrates that God has taken the process of forgiveness to completion. No unresolved loss or pain lies hidden in God's heart where it might grow into bitterness. The pain has been fully faced.

Question 8. We see in Jesus that forgiveness is one of God's central agendas. To forgive, then, is to live in solidarity, to be faithful, to be congruent with God's purposes. Whatever struggle comes with the process of forgiveness is worth it because it is part of becoming like Christ.

For more information about Christian resources for people in recovery and subscription information for STEPS, *the newsletter of the National Association for Christian Recovery, we invite you to write to:*

The National Association for Christian Recovery
P.O. Box 11095
Whittier, California 90603

LIFE RECOVERY GUIDES FROM INTER-VARSITY PRESS
By Dale and Juanita Ryan

Recovery from Abuse. Does the nightmare of abuse ever end? After emotional, verbal and/
or physical abuse how can you develop secure relationships? Recovery is difficult but possible.
This guide will help you turn to God as you put the broken pieces of your life back together
again. Six studies, 64 pages, 1158-3.

Recovery from Addictions. Addictions have always been part of the human predicament.
Chemicals, food, people, sex, work, spending, gambling, religious practices and more can en-
slave us. This guide will help you find the wholeness and restoration that God offers to those
who are struggling with addictions. Six studies, 64 pages, 1155-9.

Recovery from Bitterness. Sometimes forgiveness gets blocked, stuck, restrained and entangled. We find our hearts turning toward bitterness and revenge. Our inability to forgive
can make us feel like spiritual failures. This guide will help us find the strength to change
bitterness into forgiveness. Six studies, 64 pages, 1154-0.

Recovery from Codependency. The fear, anger and helplessness people feel when someone
they love is addicted can lead to desperate attempts to take care of, or control, the loved one.
Both the addicted person's behavior and the frenzied codependent behavior progress in a
destructive downward spiral of denial and blame. This guide will help you to let go of over-
responsibility and entrust the people you love to God. Six studies, 64 pages, 1156-7.

Recovery from Distorted Images of God. In a world of sin and hate it is difficult for us
to understand who the God of love is. These distortions interfere with our ability to express
our feelings to God and to trust him. This guide helps us to identify the distortions we have
and to come to a new understanding of who God is. Six studies, 64 pages, 1152-4.

Recovery from Family Dysfunctions. Dysfunctional patterns of relating learned early in
life affect all of our relationships. We trust God and others less than we wish. This guide
offers healing from the pain of the past and acceptance into God's family. Six studies, 64
pages, 1151-6.

Recovery from Loss. Disappointment, unmet expectations, physical or emotional illness and
death are all examples of losses that occur in our lives. Working through grief does not help
us to forget what we have lost, but it does help us grow in understanding, compassion and
courage in the midst of loss. This guide will show you how to receive the comfort God offers.
Six studies, 64 pages, 1157-5.

Recovery from Shame. Shame is a social experience. Whatever its source, shame causes
people to see themselves as unlovable, unworthy and irreparable. This guide will help you to
reform your self-understanding in the light of God's unconditional acceptance. Six studies, 64
pages, 1153-2.